Nora the Naturalist's Animals

Minibeasts

W
FRANKLIN WATTS
LONDON•SYDNEY

Franklin Watts
First published in Great Britain in 2015 by The Watts Publishing Group

Designed and illustrated by David West

Dewey number 595.71
HB ISBN 978 1 4451 4495 5

Printed in Malaysia

Franklin Watts
An imprint of
Hachette Children's Group
Part of The Watts Publishing Group
Carmelite House
50 Victoria Embankment
London EC4Y 0DZ

An Hachette UK Company
www.hachette.co.uk

www.franklinwatts.co.uk

NORA THE NATURALIST'S ANIMALS MINIBEASTS
was produced for Franklin Watts by
David West Children's Books, 6 Princeton Court, 55 Felsham Road, London SW15 1AZ

Nora the Naturalist says:
I will tell you something more about the animal.

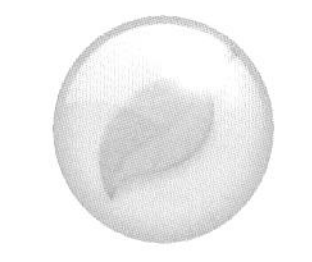

Learn what this animal eats.

Where in the world is the animal found?

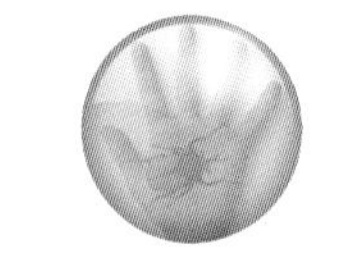

Its size is revealed!

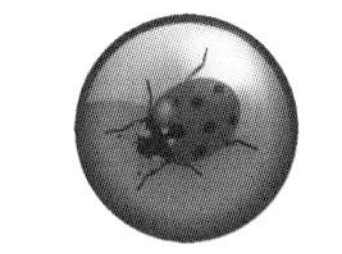

What animal group is it – mammal, bird, reptile, amphibian, insect, or something else?

Interesting facts.

Contents

Beetles

Beetles come in a variety of shapes and colours, from red ladybirds and glowing fireflies to giant horned beetles. Like all insects they have a hard outer layer, called an exoskeleton.

Ladybird

Stag beetles

Nora the Naturalist says:
Beetles have two pairs of wings. One set has become a hardened case that protects the second set of wings when they are not flying.

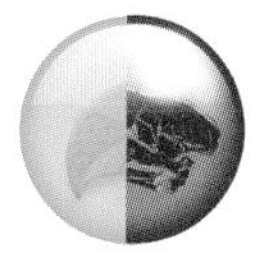

Some beetles feed on dead animal and plant matter; some feed on other animals; some feed on dung and others on fungi. Some types choose particular plants; others eat a wide range of plants.

Beetles are found all around the world, except in the seas and at the poles.

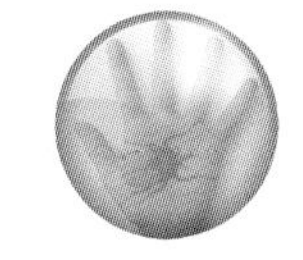

Beetles range in size from less than a millimetre to **tropical** giants of more than 15.2 centimetres.

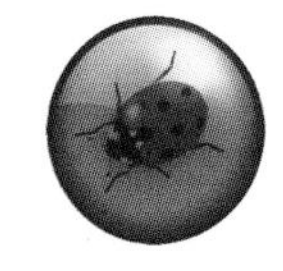

Beetles belong to the group of animals called insects.

There are around a million different types of beetles. Some are pests that can destroy trees. Others, like the ladybird, are gardeners' friends. They eat pests such as aphids.

Fireflies

Woodlice and millipedes feed on dead plant matter. Centipedes eat worms, reptiles, amphibians, small mammals, bats and birds.

Both these minibeasts are found all over the world except in the oceans and at the poles.

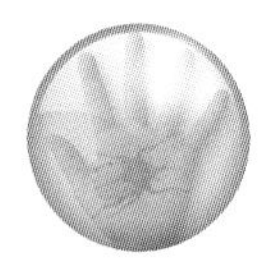

Centipedes range from less than a few millimetres long to about 30 centimetres. Woodlice range from 3–30 millimetres.

Nora the Naturalist says:
Woodlice belong to the same family as crabs and lobsters. They are the only species of crustacean that does not live in water.

Woodlice are **crustaceans**. Centipedes have their own grouping. Both are members of the **arthropod** family, which have exoskeletons.

Woodlice have other names, such as armadillo bugs, boat-builders, roly-polys, chuggypigs and pill bugs.

Many Legs

Some minibeasts have lots of legs. They include centipedes, woodlice and millipedes. Some centipedes have less than 20 legs, others have more than 100!

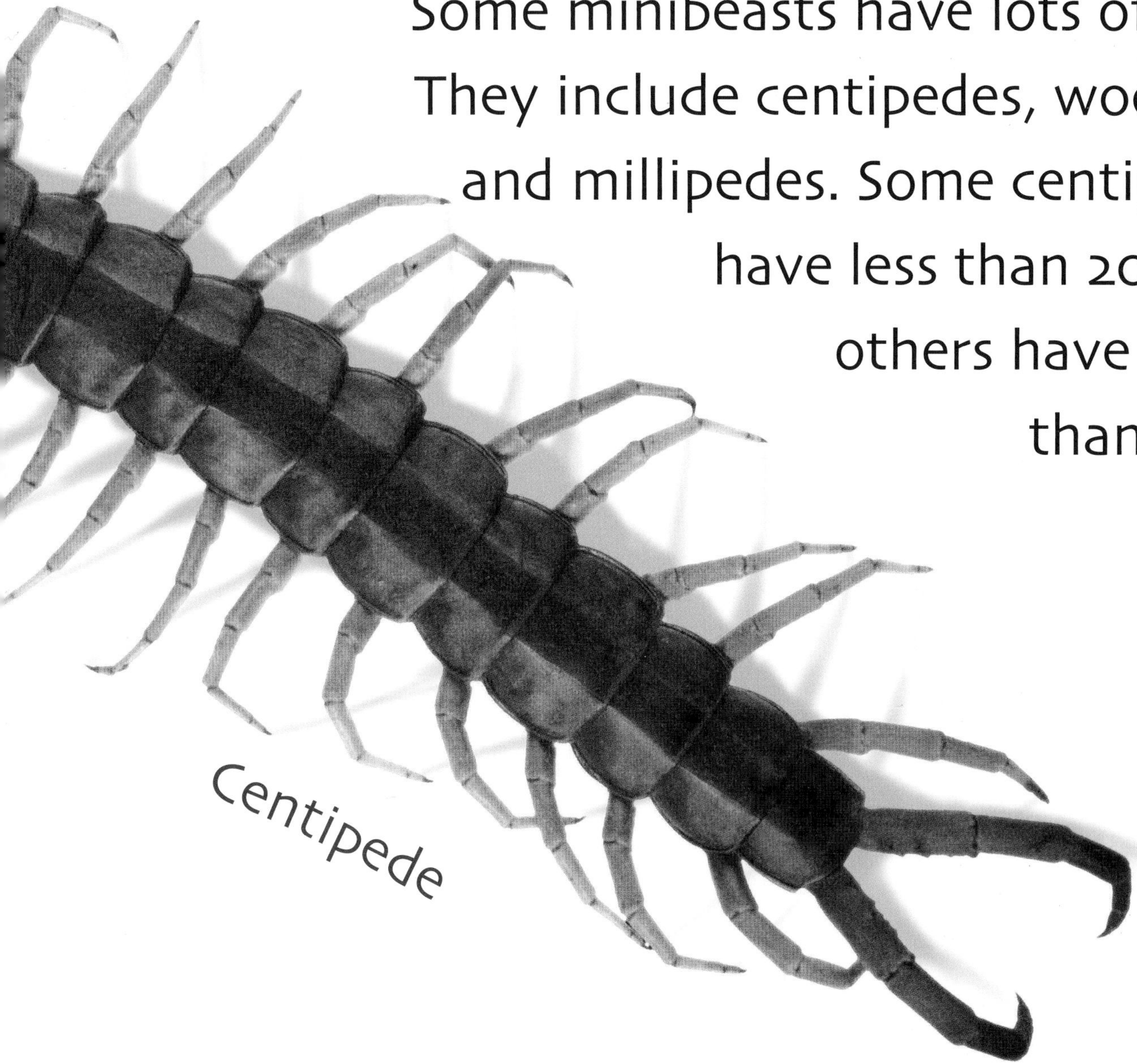

Centipede

Arachnids

All members of this arthropod family have eight legs. There are more than 100,000 different species, including spiders, scorpions, harvestmen, ticks and mites.

Spider

Arachnids are mostly meat eaters. They eat insects and other small animals. Their **digestive juices** turn their prey into 'soup', which they suck up.

Spiders and scorpions are found all over the world except at the North and South Poles, and in the sea.

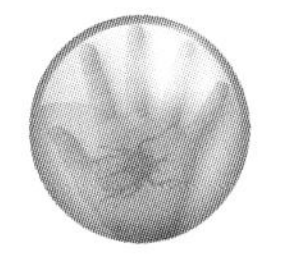

Some species of spiders have a leg span of up to 30 centimetres. Scorpions can grow up to 20 centimetres long.

Arachnids are arthropods.

Scorpions use a stinger at the end of their tail to inject venom into their prey.

Scorpion

Nora the Naturalist says:
Spiders lay eggs from which baby spiders hatch. Scorpions give birth to live young. The mother carries them around on her back until they are old enough to fend for themselves.

Nora the Naturalist says:
Most butterflies are active during the day and most moths are active during the night.

Moths

Butterflies

With a few exceptions, butterflies and moths feed on **nectar** from flowers.

They are found on every continent except Antarctica. There is even a species that lives in the Arctic.

The largest butterfly is the birdwing, which has a 30-centimetre wingspan. The Atlas moth has a wingspan of 28 centimetres.

Butterflies and moths are insects. They are members of the group called Lepidoptera.

Both moths and butterflies lay eggs that hatch into caterpillars. They then change into a **chrysalis** from which the winged adult emerges.

and Butterflies

Some of the most colourful minibeasts are these beautiful winged insects. Their brightly patterned wings are made of thousands of tiny scales.

Birdwing butterfly

Moth

Atlas moth

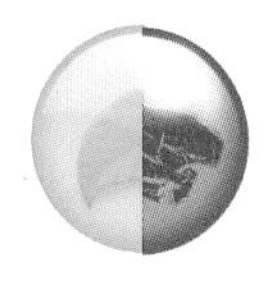

Bees feed on nectar from flowers and turn some of the nectar into honey. Wasps and hornets eat all sorts of things from fruit to insects, even including bees.

Wasps and bees are found all over the world except in the polar regions.

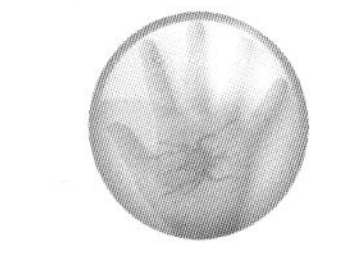

The largest bees grow up to 3.9 centimetres long. Some species of hornet can reach up to 5.5 centimetres in length.

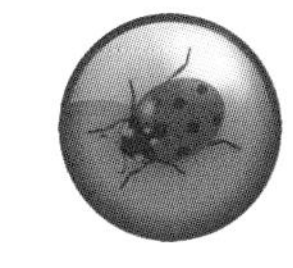

Bees and wasps are insects.

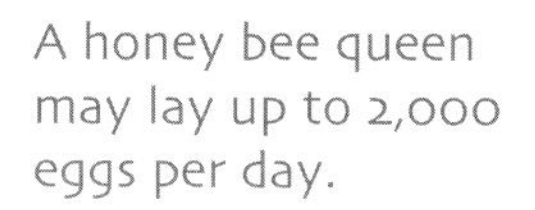

A honey bee queen may lay up to 2,000 eggs per day.

Honey bee

Bumblebee

Nora the Naturalist says:
Bumblebees live in colonies of 50 to 200 bees. They live in holes that have already been made, such as old mouse nests.

Bees and Wasps

Bees are flying insects closely related to wasps. Honey bees and wasps live in large nests. The bees make their nests with wax produced by the workers. Wasps and hornets make paper nests from chewed wood.

Noisy Bugs

Some minibeasts are very noisy. Crickets make a chirping sound by rubbing their back legs against their wings. Cicadas use special parts in their abdomen to make their 'songs'.

Nora the Naturalist says:
A certain type of grasshopper changes its colour and behaviour when its numbers increase. It is called a locust and can cause a great deal of damage to crops.

Grasshopper

Cicadas suck sap from various species of tree. Grasshoppers eat grasses, leaves and cereal crops.

Cicadas like warm climates and are mostly found in tropical regions. Grasshoppers live throughout the world, except at the extremely cold North Pole and South Pole.

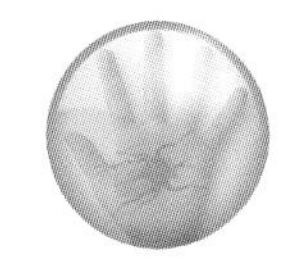

Grasshoppers grow to around 5 centimetres. Some tropical species of cicada can reach 15 centimetres.

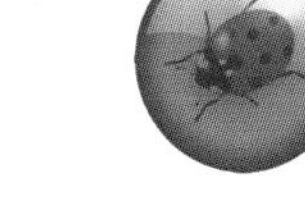

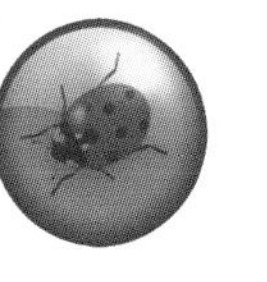

Both grasshoppers and cicadas are insects.

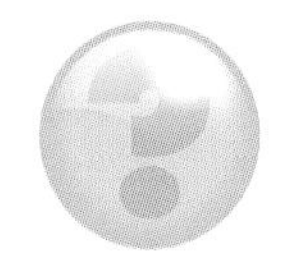

Cicadas live underground as nymphs for most of their lives, as deep as 2.6 metres below ground.

Cicada

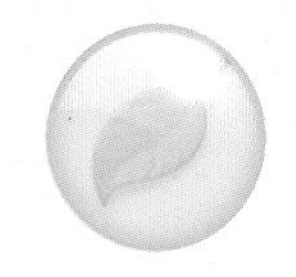

Crane fly maggots, called leatherjackets, eat the stems of plants. The adults rarely eat. Flies eat liquid food.

Crane fly

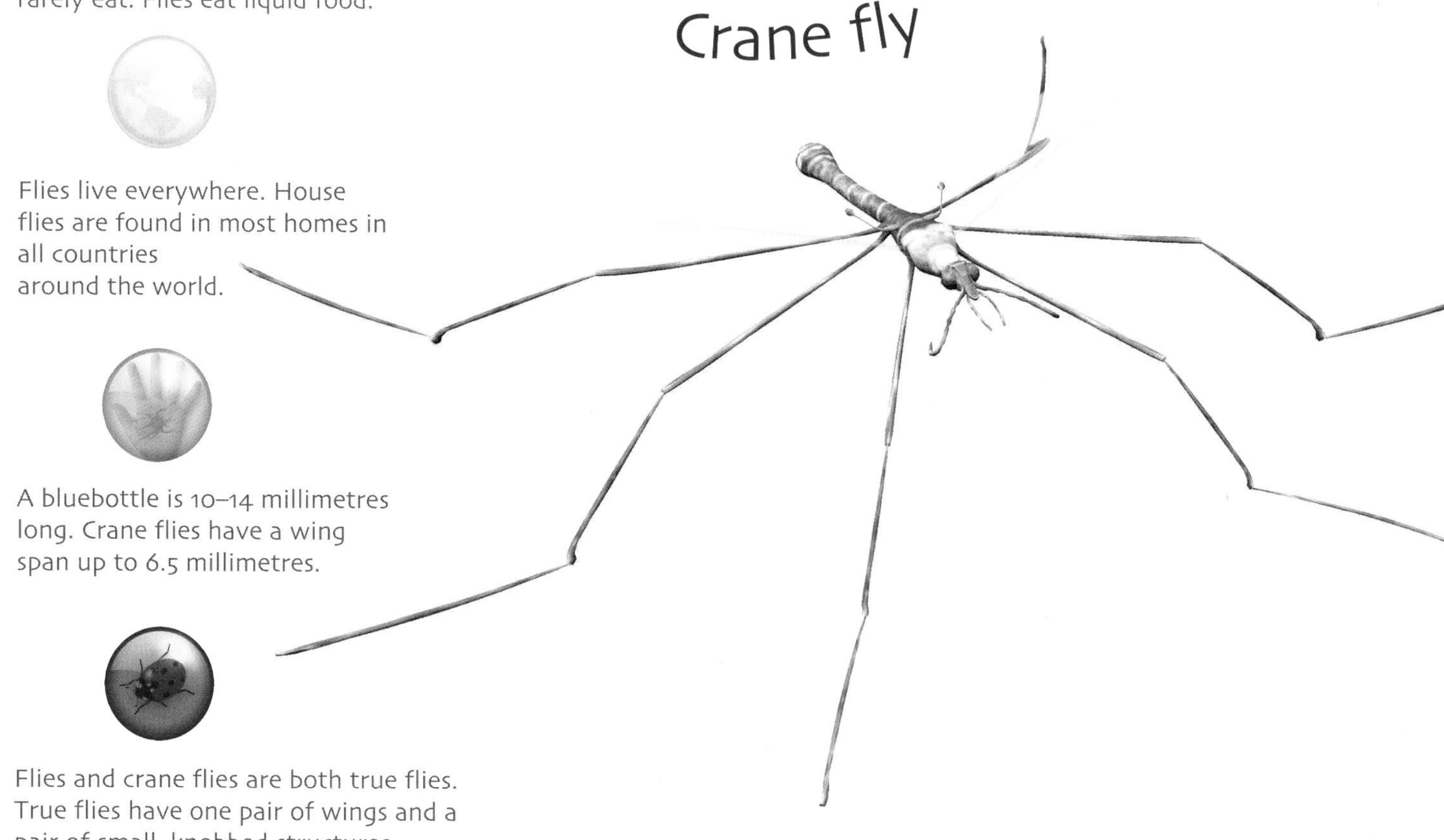

Flies live everywhere. House flies are found in most homes in all countries around the world.

A bluebottle is 10–14 millimetres long. Crane flies have a wing span up to 6.5 millimetres.

Flies and crane flies are both true flies. True flies have one pair of wings and a pair of small, knobbed structures instead of a second pair of wings.

True flies' single pair of wings makes them different from other insects with 'fly' in their name, such as dragonflies, which have two pairs of wings.

Flies

Flies are insects with one pair of wings. They have huge eyes, which can detect the smallest movement. This makes them very difficult to catch.

Bluebottles

Maggots

Nora the Naturalist says:
Flies start life as maggots after hatching from eggs. They then go through a pupa stage before turning into a fly.

Worms

Earthworms have no eyes or legs. They are made up of ring-like **segments** that have short, stiff hairs growing from them. As a segment expands and contracts, the hairs stick to the soil, helping it to move forwards.

Nora the Naturalist says:
Earthworms are very good for the soil. They break down plant matter, making the soil richer to grow things in.

Earthworm

Earthworms eat dead plant matter and soil.

The common earthworm can be found in Europe, North America and Western Asia.

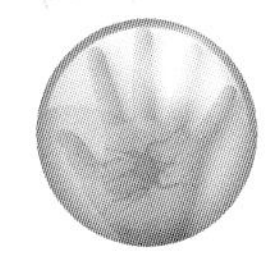

Earthworms can grow up to an amazing 35 centimetres long.

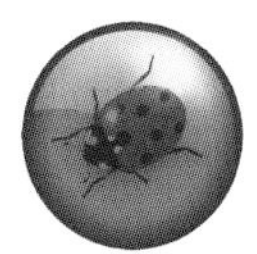

Earthworms are members of the **annelid** family.

Earthworms improve soil by making worm holes. These holes let air in and water out of the soil

Snails are usually plant eaters, but there are some species that eat meat.

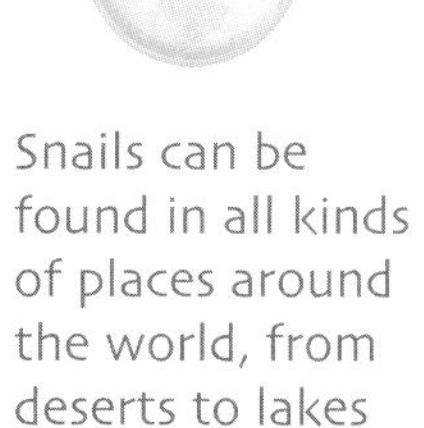

Snails can be found in all kinds of places around the world, from deserts to lakes and oceans. They are not found at the poles.

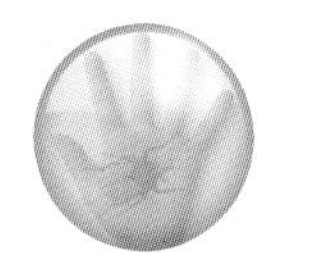

Africa has the largest snails. Their shells can measure up to 18 centimetres across.

Snails are members of the mollusc family. They are closely related to slugs.

Garden snails can be eaten and are a popular meal in some countries, like France.

Snail

Snails

Garden snails are often thought of as pests. Their messy trails of mucus and their taste for greens has made them enemies of the gardener. They are often seen after rain.

Nora the Naturalist says:
When it's dry snails retreat into their shells and seal the entrance closed.

Earwigs

Earwigs are only active at night. During the day they often hide in small, damp crevices. They feed on a wide variety of insects and plants.

Earwigs eat other insects as well as plant matter.

Earwigs are found throughout the Americas, Africa, Eurasia, Australia and New Zealand.

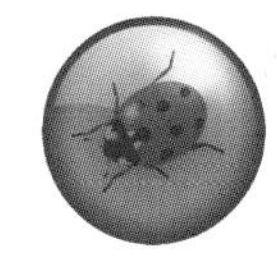

Earwigs are insects.

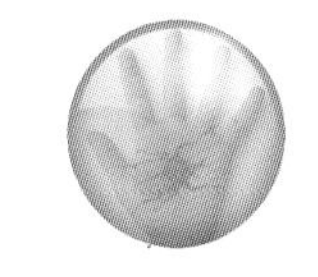

Some earwigs, such as the Saint Helena earwig, can grow to 8 centimetres long.

Earwigs use their pincers to capture prey and to defend themselves.

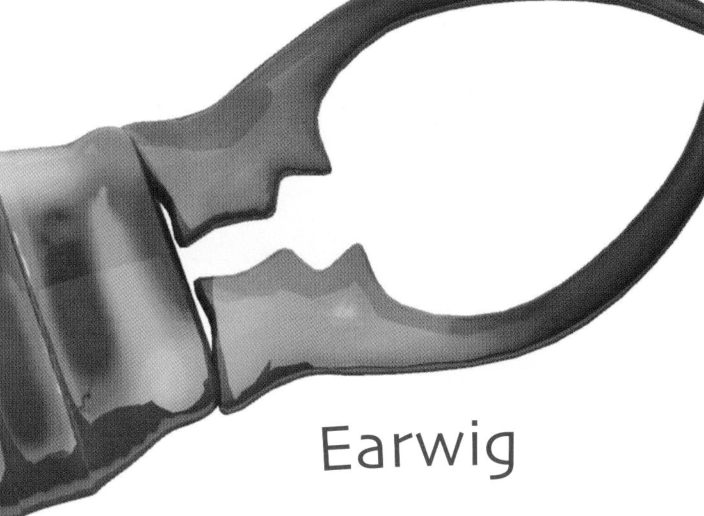

Earwig

Nora the Naturalist says:
Female earwigs are good mothers. Unlike most insects they look after their young for several weeks after they have hatched from their eggs.

Glossary

annelid
A family of worm species, including earthworms.

arthropod
An animal without a backbone that has an exoskeleton.

chrysalis
The hard case of an insect before it becomes a moth or butterfly.

crustaceans
A group of arthropods, such as crabs and lobsters.

digestive juices
Fluids to break down food.

nectar
Sugary liquid in flowers.

segments
Rings on an earthworm.

tropical
A hot and humid climate.

Index